THE LONGMAN PICTURE DICTIONARY

CANADIAN EDITION

JULIE ASHWORTH • JOHN CLARK

Longman

Published in Canada by
Éditions du Renouveau Pédagogique, Inc.
5757 Cypihot
Saint-Laurent, Quebec
Canada H4S 1R3

First published by Nelson ELT 1993

Dépôt légal : 1er trimestre 2001
Bibliothèque nationale du Québec
Bibliothèque nationale du Canada
Imprimé au Canada/Printed in Canada

ISBN 2-7613-1195-7

1234567890 FR 0543210
131195 ABCD JS-14

(Nelson ed. ISBN 0-17-556452-3 ; Addison Wesley ed. ISBN 0-582-29981-0)

Acknowledgments

The authors would like to thank the following consultants and teachers for their valuable feedback: Gwyneth Fox, Jackie Holderness, Wendy Superfine, Denise Werlé. They would also like to thank: John Blundall of the Scottish Mask and Puppet Theatre in Glasgow for the use of the puppets and masks on pages 16 and 17; Children's World, Crown Point Retail Park, Leeds, and Sportstime, Arndale Centre, Leeds for the loan of toys and equipment on pages 10 and 11.

Design: Julie Ashworth

Photos: Anton Stark

Illustrations: Julie Ashworth (pages 6, 8, 9, 20, 21, 40, 41, 42, 44, 45, 56, 57, 62); Rowan Barnes-Murphy (pages 24, 36, 37); Jerry Collins (pages 29, 57, 64); Andy Cooke (pages 25, 60, 61); John Gosler (page 63); David Parkins (pages 18, 19, 38, 39, 54, 55, 58, 59); Chris Pavely (pages 23, 24, 30, 35, 36, 39, 53, 64, 67); Valeria Petrone (52, 53); Marie José Sacré (30, 31, 32, 33); Pippa Sampson (pages 12, 13, 14, 15, 22, 23, 34, 35, 46, 47, 48, 49, 50, 51); Peter Schrank (pages 11, 28, 29, 30)

Additional artwork: Chantal Boyer (pages 22, 23, 36, 37, 39, 59); Philippe Morin (pages 34, 39, 42, 46, 47, 49, 64)

Introduction

The Longman Picture Dictionary is specially designed for use in the classroom or at home. It can equally be enjoyed by the child working alone, the child working with a parent/guardian or friend and, of course, the child in class.

The dictionary is divided into two parts. The first part is a full colour picture dictionary. Words are listed alphabetically and grouped according to topic.The second part is a complete alphabetical list of all the words in the dictionary with page references.

How to use this dictionary

To find the meaning of an English word ...

If you want to know what the word *skirt* means, look under the letter s in the word list at the back of the book. The number next to the word tells you which page the word *skirt* is on.

skateboard 35	South Korean 64
skeleton 55	soy sauce 28
ski 43	space 8
skiing 39	space ship 35
skip 43	space shuttle 35
skirt 20	spade 50
sky 50	spaghetti 29
sleep 45	Spain 64
slide 51	Spanish 64
slipper 20	speedboat 35
slow 59	spider 63

To find an English word for something ...

If you want to know the English word for an article of clothing (e.g. a skirt), look at the Contents (page 4/5) and find the relevant topic, in this case CLOTHES. Turn to page 20. Look for the picture of a skirt in the word list and you will find the English word.

To check the spelling of an English word ...

If you want to know how to spell the word *skirt*, look under the letter s in the word list or find the word on the appropriate page.

Games and activities

There are games and activities on every double-page spread which help develop skills such as sorting, spelling, counting and matching. These can be done by the child working alone (after being given some initial guidance) or, of course, as classroom activities. The beautiful illustrations with interwoven storylines and visual twists allow the pictures to be used time and again for a variety of language activities such as storytelling, pairwork, etc.

Contents

From A to Z

AdnE	letters
BMK	capital letters
fjck	lower case letters
hello goodbye	words

PUNCTUATION

,	comma
.	period
?	question mark

astronaut
balloon
broom
brush
cage
candle
cobweb
dinosaur
envelope
firework
flag
garbage can
grasshopper
hammer

igloo
jar
juggler
key
kite
ladder
letter
lobster
magnet
match
needle
newspaper
octopus
pin

queen
rainbow
rope
snowman
suitcase
telescope
turtle
umbrella
vampire
wheel
xylophone
yacht
yo-yo
zipper

- How many letters are there in the alphabet?
- How many words on this page begin with the letter **l**?
- How many letters are there in the word **xylophone**?
- What is the longest word on this page?
- Write these letters in alphabetical order:

  b e i t o n s u y a

- What are these?

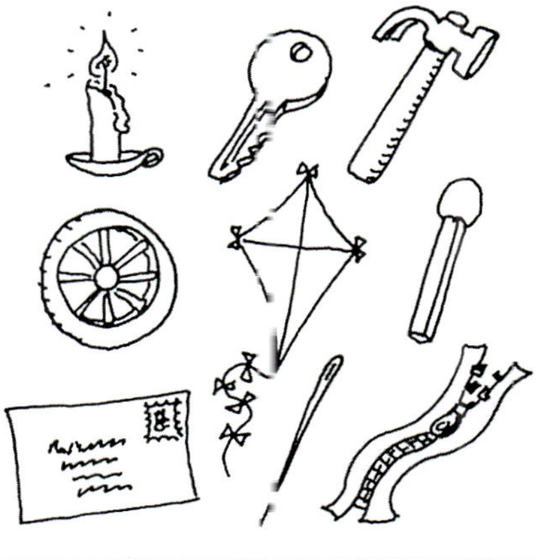

In Space

Look at the picture.

- How many squares are there?
- What colour are the stars?
- Draw a picture of a house. Use 3 triangles, 7 squares, 2 rectangles and a circle.

Look at the photographs.

- What colour is the comb?
- What colour are the pens?
- What are coins made of?
- What can you see in the photographs? Make a list.

cloth	glass	metal	paper
pigs	bottle vase	key coins	stamps envelope

COLOURS

black

blue

brown

gold

green

grey

orange

pink

purple

red

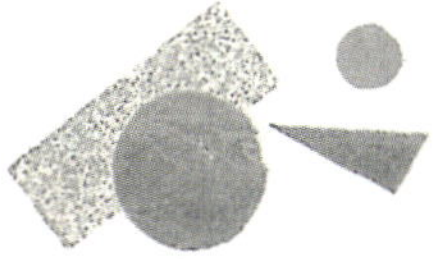
silver

white

yellow

MATERIALS

cloth

glass

metal

paper

plastic

rubber

wood

wool

SHAPES

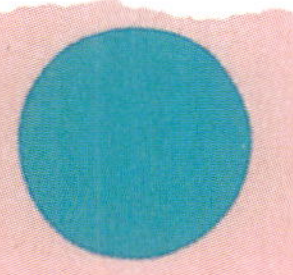
circle

square

heart

star

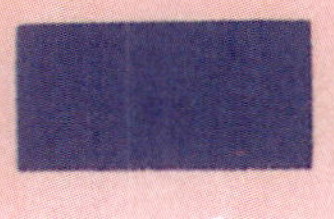
rectangle

triangle

NUMBERS

0	zero
1	one
2	two
3	three
4	four
5	five
6	six
7	seven
8	eight
9	nine
10	ten
11	eleven
12	twelve
13	thirteen
14	fourteen
15	fifteen
16	sixteen
17	seventeen
18	eighteen
19	nineteen
20	twenty
30	thirty
40	forty
50	fifty
60	sixty
70	seventy
80	eighty
90	ninety
100	a hundred
1 000	a thousand
1 000 000	a million

How Many?

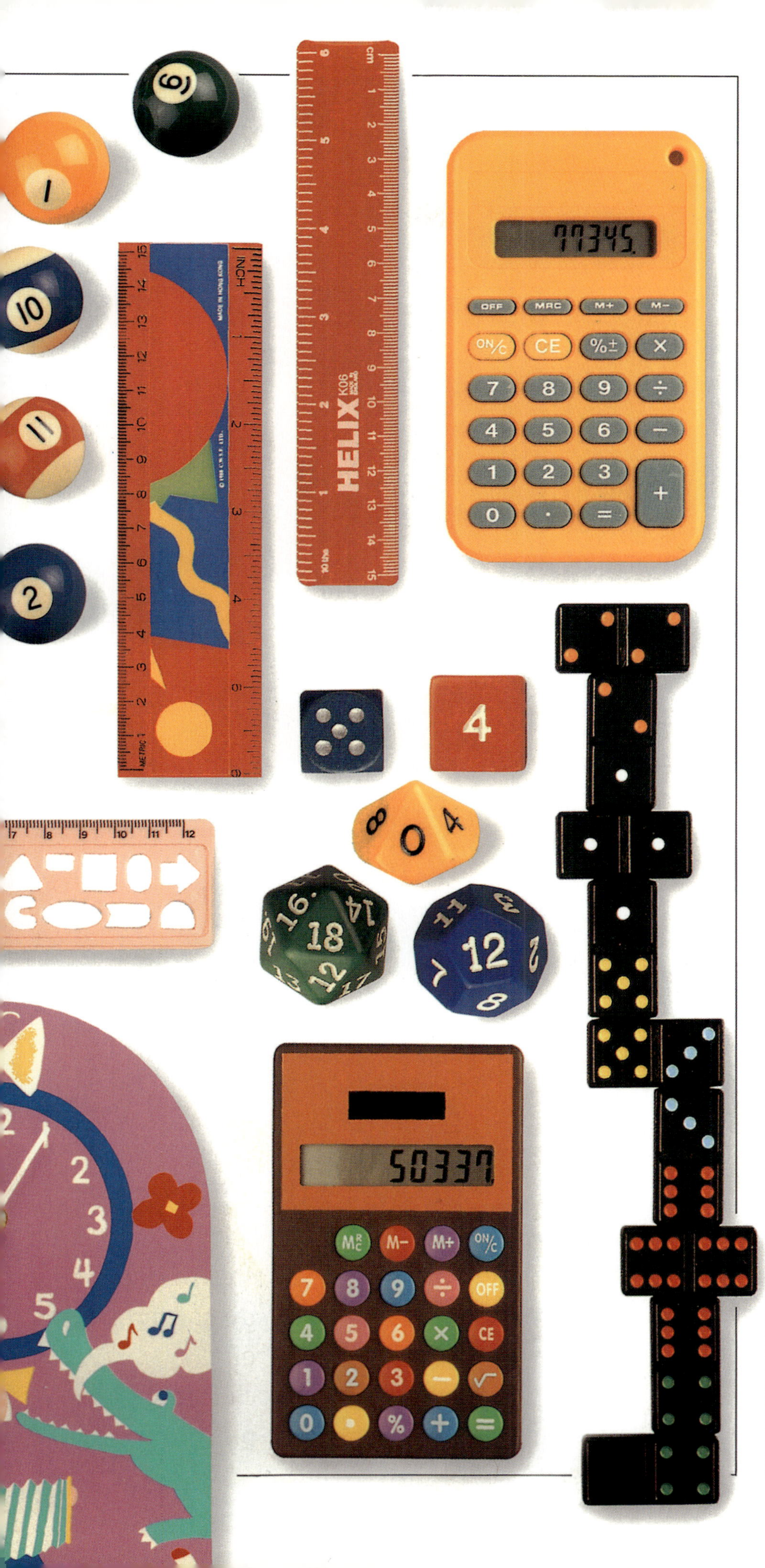

 ball

 calculator

 car

 clock

 counter

 die

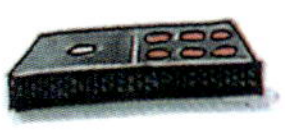 domino

 playing card

 ruler

FRACTIONS

$\frac{1}{2}$ half

$\frac{1}{4}$ quarter

- Find 7 animals in the photograph.
- Find these numbers in the photograph.
  18 57 15 300
- What numbers are on the counters?
- Count from 1 to 10 in English. Then count backwards from 10 to 1.
- How many cars are there?
  How many rulers?
  How many playing cards?
  Make a chart.

1	clock
2	calculators

A Day at School

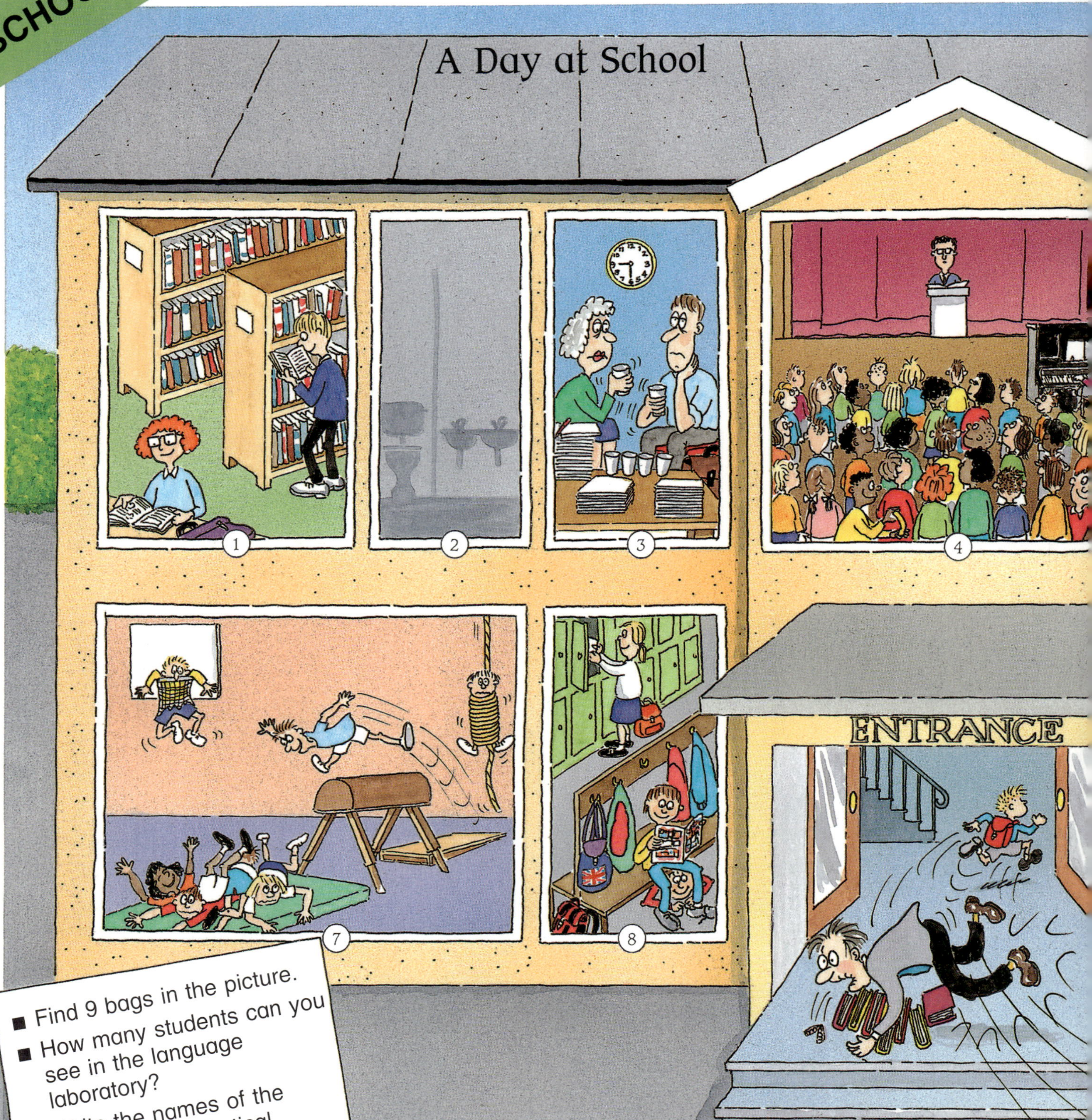

- Find 9 bags in the picture.
- How many students can you see in the language laboratory?
- Write the names of the rooms in alphabetical order.
- What is in your bag? Draw pictures and write the words.

ROOMS

1 library
2 bathroom
3 staff room
4 auditorium
5 language laboratory
6 science laboratory
7 gymnasium/gym
8 locker room
9 office
10 classroom
11 playground

SCHEDULE

	09:00 10:00	10:00 10:30	10:30 12:00	12:00 13:00	13:00 14:30	14:30 15:30
MON	Math	RECESS	English	LUNCH	Geography	Gym
TUES	Science		History		Music	Art
WED	Geography		Math		History	English

bag

crayons

eraser

notebook

pen

pencil

pencil case

pencil sharpener

ruler

In the Classroom

- Look at the words on page 15. Find each thing in the picture.
- Look at the picture. Work with a friend. Give instructions. e.g. *Point to the scissors. Point to the calculator.*
- Guess these words.

  c a _ _ _ _ _ _ _ _

  b _ _

  s _ _ _ _

  Now write the words in alphabetical order.

- bell
- binder/ Duo-Tang®
- bookcase
- box
- cabinet/ cupboard
- calculator
- cassette
- cassette player
- chair
- chalk
- chalkboard
- chalkboard eraser
- clock
- compass
- computer
- desk
- drawer
- drawing
- easel
- glue
- light
- paintbrush
- paper
- paper clip
- plant
- poster
- scales
- scissors
- Scotch tape®
- shelf
- stapler
- string
- students
- teacher
- thumbtack
- VCR
- wastebasket
- whiteboard

Puppets and Masks

- Find 5 words beginning with the letter **f**.
- Look at the puppets and masks. Count the ears. Count the eyes. Count the teeth.
- Which mask has long eyebrows?
- Which mask has the biggest ears?
- Write these words in alphabetical order:

  beard body back bald
- Draw a puppet or mask with a long nose, big eyes and curly hair. Label your picture.

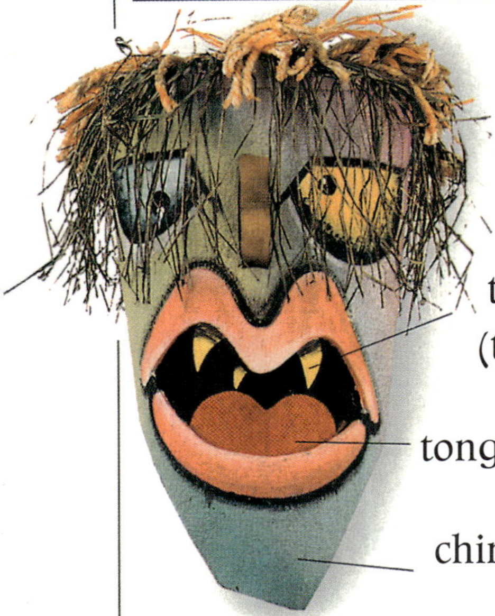

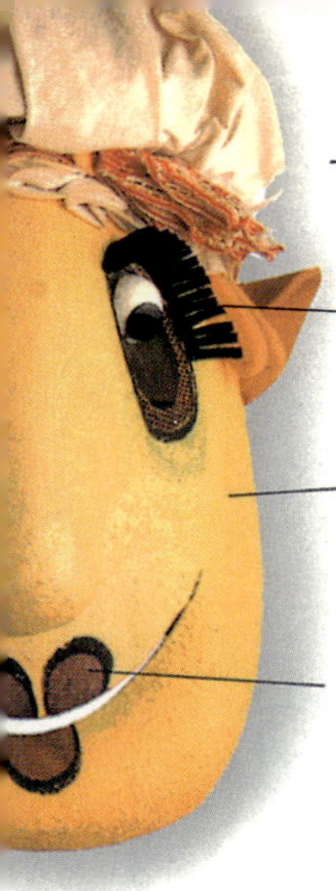
eyelash
cheek
lip

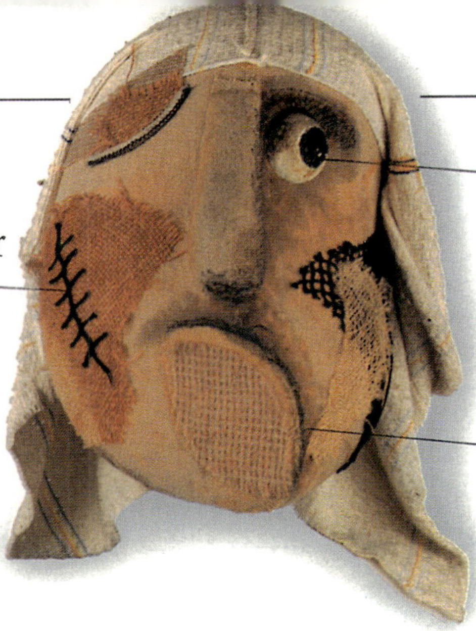
scar
eye
mouth

neck
shoulder
chest
thumb
arm
finger
hand
toe

forehead
ear
nose
mustache

HAIR

bald
blond
curly
dark
straight
redheaded

The Monster Family

grandparents
grandfather/ grandpa
granddaughter
grandmother/ grandma
granddaughter
parents
father/ dad/ daddy
daughter
mother/ mom/ mommy
daughter
brothers
sister
aunts
niece
uncles
niece
cousin
cousin

PEOPLE

children

baby

boy

girl

adults

man

woman

- How many different monsters are there?
- Rearrange the letters to make words.

ecien	**phenwe**
clune	**uatn**
itsesr	**oretbhr**
heomtr	**rehfta**

- The purple monster is called Plum. Give the other monsters a name.
- How many cousins does Plum have? Who is Plum's grandmother? Write some more questions.
- Find 8 different words with 6 letters.
- Make a poster of yourself and your family. Use photos or draw pictures. Label the pictures.

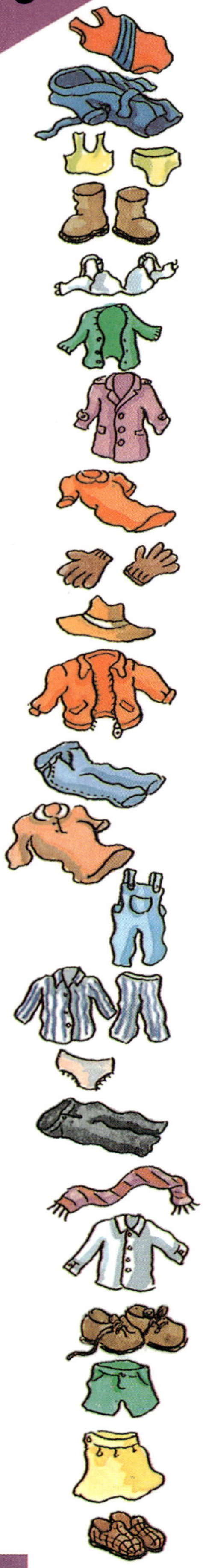

bathing suit/ swimsuit
bathrobe
bikini
boots
bra
cardigan
coat
dress
gloves
hat
jacket
jeans
nightie/ nightgown
overalls
pyjamas
panties
pants
scarf
shirt
shoes
shorts
skirt
slippers

The Campsite

- Find these things in the picture.

  What are they called in English?
- Work with a friend. Ask some questions about the picture.
  e.g. *Who's wearing a red dress?*
  Who's wearing overalls?

sneakers/
running shoes

socks

sweater

sweatsuit

sweatshirt

tie

tights

T-shirt

underpants

undershirt

uniform

JEWELLERY

bracelet
earrings
necklace
ring

barrette
belt
button
glasses
pocket
ribbon
shoelace

Animals of the World

- How many animals are there on the map?
- Which animals live on 3 different continents? Guess. Then check.
- Which animals have wings?
- Work with a friend. Think of an animal. Ask your friend to guess the animal.
  e.g. *Is it brown?*
  Does it have 4 legs?
  Does it live in Africa?

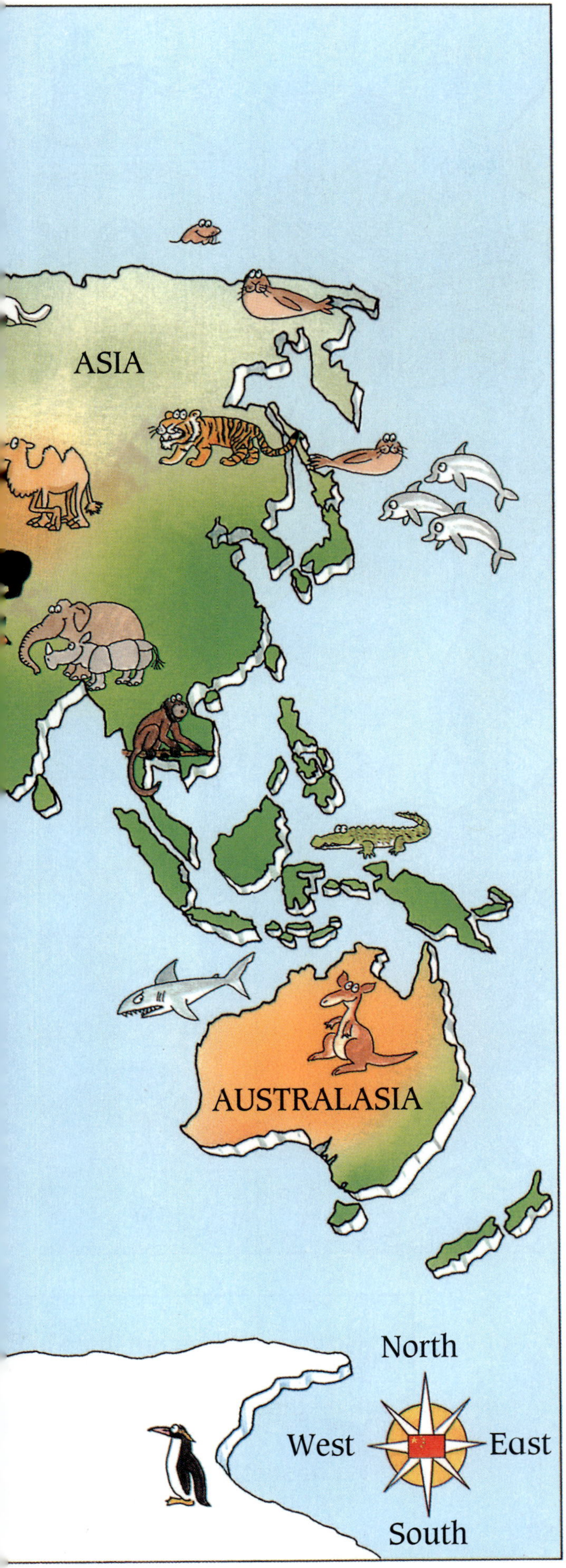

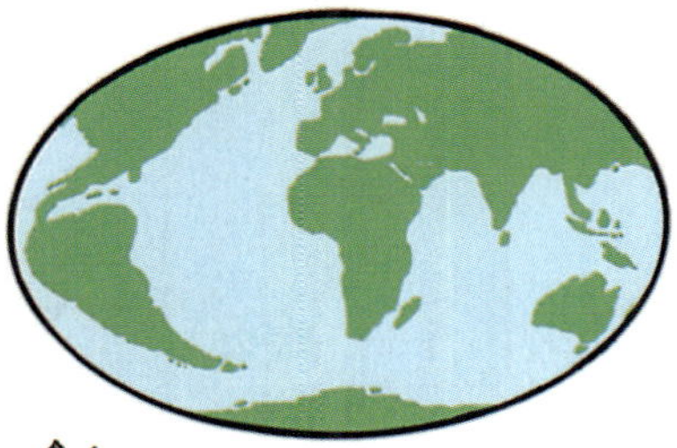

	AFRICA	AMERICA	ANTARCTICA	ASIA	AUSTRALASIA	EUROPE
bat	●	●		●	●	●
bear		●		●		●
beaver		●		●		●
camel	●			●		
crocodile	●	●		●	●	
dolphin	●	●		●	●	●
elephant	●			●		
fox	●	●		●		●
giraffe	●					
gorilla	●					
hippopotamus	●					
kangaroo					●	
lion	●			●		
lizard	●	●		●	●	●
monkey	●	●		●		
moose		●		●		●
octopus	●	●		●	●	●
ostrich	●					
owl	●	●		●	●	●
pelican	●	●		●	●	●
penguin	●	●	●		●	
polar bear		●				
rhinoceros	●			●		
seal	●	●	●	●	●	●
shark	●	●		●	●	●
snake	●	●		●	●	●
tiger				●		
whale	●	●	●	●	●	●
wolf	●	●		●		●
zebra	●					

Pets

1	canary	6	guinea pig	11	parrot
2	cat	7	hamster	12	puppy
3	dog	8	kitten	13	rabbit
4	fish	9	mouse	14	rat
5	frog	10	parakeet	15	turtle

- How many mice are there in th pet shop?
- Find these things in the pet shop:

  a basket **a fish tank**
  a cage **a kennel**

Farm Animals

How many birds are there on the farm and in the pet store?

How many chicks are there on the farm?

What is a young cow called?

What colour is the pig?

1 bull
2 calf
3 chick
4 cow
5 donkey
6 duck
7 goat
8 goose
9 hen
10 horse
11 lamb
12 pig
13 piglet
14 rooster
15 sheep

Fruit and Vegetables

- Find 10 words on this page with 6 letters.
- How many green vegetables are there?
- Work with a friend. Describe a fruit or vegetable.
  e.g. *It's a long orange vegetable.*
  Ask your friend to guess the name.
- Ask your friends:
  Do you like potatoes?
  Do you like apples?
  What's your favourite fruit?
  What's your favourite vegetable?
- Make a list of fruit and vegetables.

fruit	vegetables
apple apricot	asparagus

apple

apricot

broccoli

Brussels sprouts

celery

cherries

coconut

grapefruit

grapes

green beans

leek

melon

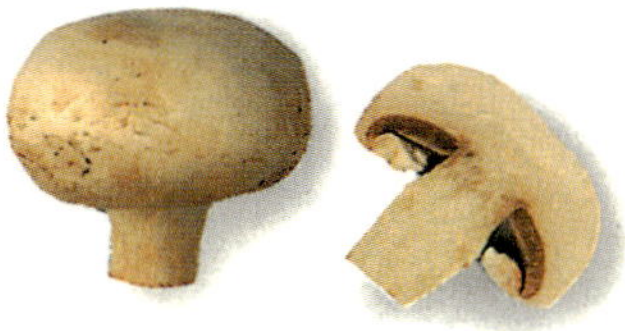
mushroom

onion

orange

papaya

plum

potato

raspberry

spinach

strawberry

asparagus
avocado
banana
beet
cabbage
carrot
cauliflower
corn
cucumber
eggplant
emon
lettuce
lime
mango
peach
pear
peas
pepper
pineapple
tomato
turnip
watermelon
zucchini

A Party

- How many glasses are there on the table?
- Find 7 things beginning with the letter **s**.
- Close the dictionary. Can you remember what is on the table?
- What are these?

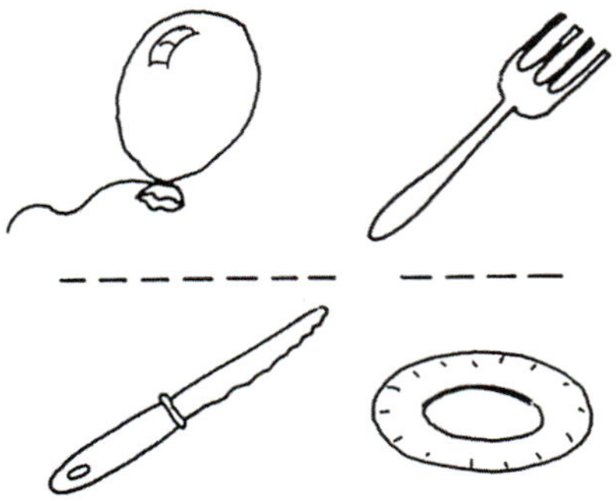

_ _ _ _ _ _ _   _ _ _ _

_ _ _ _ _   _ _ _ _ _

- What did you eat and drink yesterday? Make a list.

breakfast	lunch	supper
orange juice cornflakes	salad	chicken rice

DRINKS

beer

coffee

fruit juice

milk

tea

water

wine

ON THE TABLE

ketchup

mustard

pepper

salt

soya sauce

sugar

MEAL TIMES

- breakfast
- lunch
- supper/dinner

BREAKFAST

- bacon
- butter
- cereal
- croissant
- eggs
- jam
- toast
- yogurt

LUNCH & SUPPER

- beef
- bread
- cheese
- chicken
- fish
- French fries
- ham
- rice
- salad
- sausage
- soup
- spaghetti

city

town

apartments

house

OUTSIDE

1 antenna
2 balcony
3 chimney
4 front yard
5 garage
6 roof

Upstairs

bathroom

 bathtub

 bed

 blanket

 carpet

 comforter

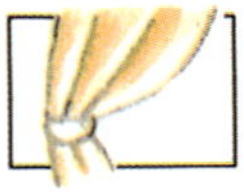 curtain

 lamp

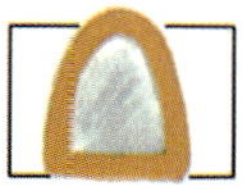 mirror

 picture

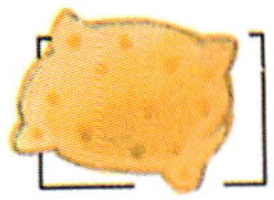 pillow

 plug

 rug

 sheets

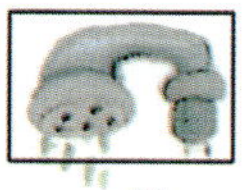 shower

 sink

 soap

 tap

 toilet

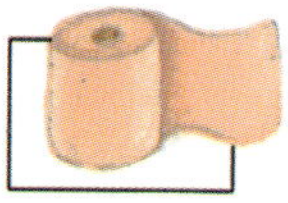 toilet paper

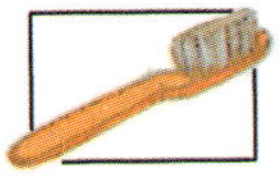 toothbrush

 toothpaste

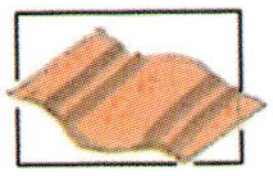 towel

 vase

 wardrobe

- Find 10 coins in the picture.
- Find 5 red things in the picture.
- Translate these words:

  bathtub blanket curtain bed carpet

  Write them in alphabetical order in your language.
- Which things are in the bedroom and which things are in the bathroom? Make a list.

bedroom	bathroom
bed blanket	bathtub

- Find 10 keys in the picture.
- Find 3 things in the kitchen beginning with the letter **m**.
- Find 3 things in the living room beginning with the letter **p**.
- Close your book. Can you remember what is in the living room?
- What colour is the kettle?
- Write the names of 5 things that are in the living room and in the kitchen too.

armchair

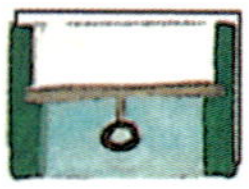
blind

bottle

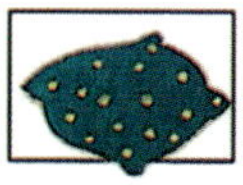
cushion

dishwasher

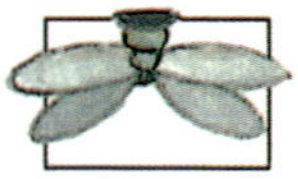
fan

freezer

fridge/refrigerator

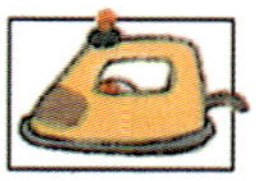
iron

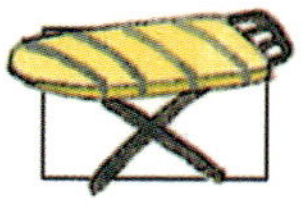
ironing board

jar

kettle

living/dining room

ON THE TABLE

 bowl

 cup

 fork

 glass

 knife

 mug

 plate

 saucer

 spoon

 tablecloth

 teapot

 microwave

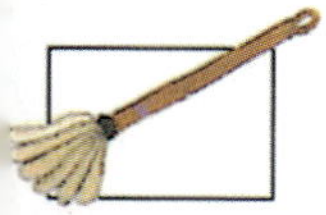 mop

 oven

 pan

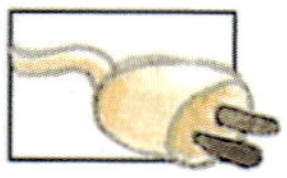 plug

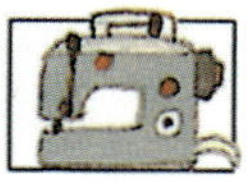 sewing machine

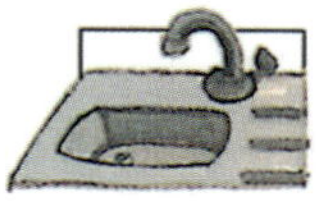 sink

 sofa/couch

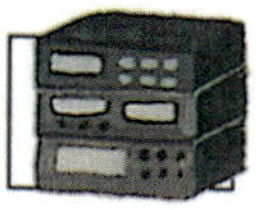 sound system

 stool

 stove

 switch

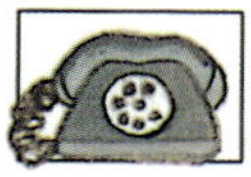 telephone

 television/TV

 toaster

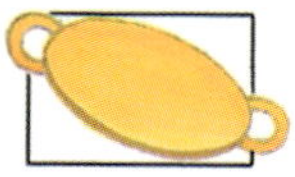 tray

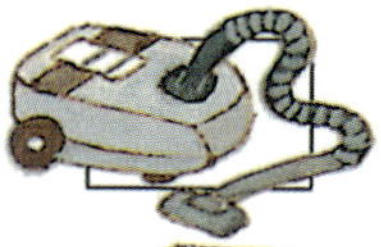 vacuum cleaner

 washing machine

Air, Land and Sea

- How many animals are there in the picture?
- Find these things in the picture:

  a helmet
  a gas pump
  a fish
  a ladder

- Look at the words on page 35. Work with a friend. Ask some questions about spelling.
  e.g. *How do you spell* plane?
  Check your friend's answers.

airplane/plane
ambulance
baby carriage
balloon
barge
bicycle/bike
blimp
boat
bus
canoe
car
ferry
fire engine
hang-glider
helicopter
hovercraft
motorcycle
parachute
police car
rocket
roller skates
school bus
scooter
ship
skateboard
space shuttle
speedboat
streetcar
stroller
submarine
tank
trailer
train
tricycle
truck
van
wheelchair
yacht

Ruby's Room

TOYS

- ball
- bat
- building blocks
- cards
- clown
- computer game
- doll
- dollhouse
- games
- jigsaw puzzle
- skipping rope
- paints
- robot
- skates
- stuffed animals
- teddy bear
- train set
- walkie-talkies

PERSONAL THINGS

- books
- camera
- CD player
- comb
- diary
- flashlight
- hairbrush
- hairdryer
- headphones
- make-up
- money
- piggy bank
- purse
- sportsbag
- track shoes
- Walkman®
- wallet
- watch

THINGS TO COLLECT

- autographs
- badges
- coins
- comic books
- medals
- models
- photographs
- postcards
- stamps

■ Find 8 things in the picture beginning with the letter **c**.

■ Which of these things is not in the picture?

a car
a doll
a medal
a purse
a robot
a watch

■ Connect the words.

computer	**rope**
skipping	**puzzle**
comic	**dryer**
photo	**game**
jigsaw	**set**
hair	**album**
train	**book**

■ Work with a friend. Ask some questions about the picture.
e.g. *Where's the purse? What colour's the comb?*

Music

INSTRUMENTS

1	banjo	8	guitar	15	synthesizer
2	cello	9	harmonica	16	tambourine
3	clarinet	10	harp	17	triangle
4	cymbals	11	maracas	18	trombone
5	double bass	12	piano	19	trumpet
6	drums	13	recorder	20	violin
7	flute	14	saxophone	21	xylophone

- Which instruments do you blow?
- Cover the words on page 38. Can you remember the name of the instruments? Check your answers and try again.
- What is the difference betwee a double bass and a cello?

Sport

baseball

basketball

football

gymnastics

hockey

horse riding

judo

skating

skiing

soccer

swimming

table tennis

tennis

track and field

- In which sports do you use these things?

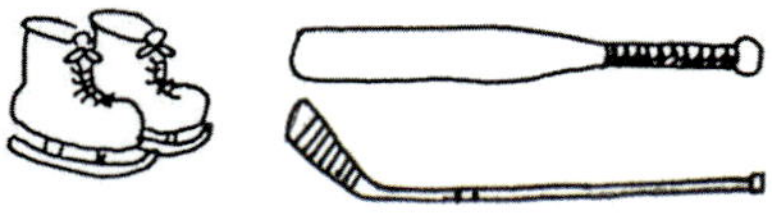

- Rearrange the letters and make words.

saelabbl **llabbtaeks**
nnstie **lfloaobt**

The Action Board Game

This is a board game for two or more players.

You need:

Rules

1 Put your counters on START.
2 Throw the die. Move your counter.
3 When you land on a square, do the action, e.g. cough if you land on square 4.
4 If you do the action wrongly, miss a turn.
5 The first player to reach FINISH is the winner.

■ Find these things in the pictures:

a bottle **a pencil**
a lamp **a stool**

■ Say this rhyme and do the actions.

Point to the ceiling,
Touch the floor.
Open the window,
And close the door.

■ What are the boys and girls doing? Make a list.

boys	girls
close	blow clap

close
4
cough
5
crawl
6
cry
7
dance
jump
11
hop
10
fall
9
drop
8
draw
read
20
run
21
MISS A TURN
22
scratch
23
scream
smile
27
sit down
26
sing
25
shout
24
shake
wave
36
whisper
37
whistle
38
write
FINISH

In the Playground

1 argue
2 bite
3 bounce
4 build
5 buy
6 carry
7 catch
8 climb
9 copy
10 dig
11 dive
12 drive
13 fight
14 fish
15 fly
16 give
17 hide
18 hit
19 hug
20 juggle
21 kick
22 kiss
23 knock
24 lift
25 measure
26 paint
27 pull
28 push
29 ride
30 roller-skate
31 ski
32 skip
33 swim
34 take
35 tear
36 throw

- How many children are there in the playground? How many boys? How many girls?
- What are they doing?

He's throwing a ball.

She's juggling.

They're arguing.

Point to the children in the picture. Ask your friend:
What's he doing?
What's she doing?

- Pick a number from 1 to 36. Say the number. Ask your friend to mime the action.
- There are 5 letters in the picture. Find the letters and make a word.
- Ask your friends:
  Can you swim? *Can you climb?*
  Can you ski? *Can you juggle?*
  Draw a graph.

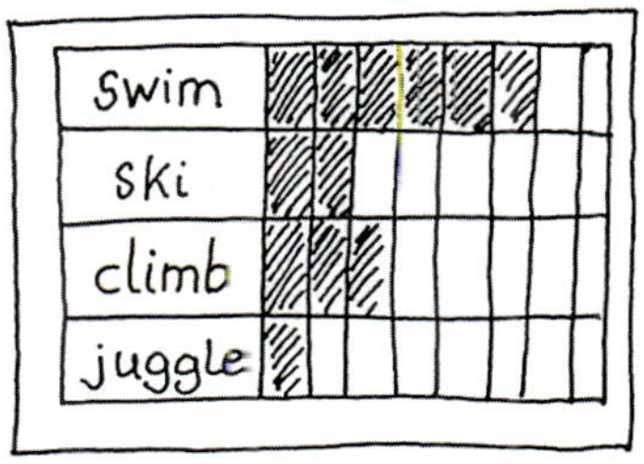

In the Home

break

brush

clean

do the dishes

dream

drink

get dressed

get up

go to bed

peel

pour

put on

sweep

take a bath

take a shower

wake up

wash

watch

comb

cook

cut

dry

eat

fix

iron

knit

listen

sew

sleep

stretch

take off

tie

weigh

yawn

- Find these things in the pictures:

  an apple **an iron**
  a cake **a towel**

- All of these words are verbs. Which words are also nouns?

  comb drink eat iron listen

- Mime one of the actions. Ask a friend to guess what you are doing.

The Town

- How many animals are there in the picture?
- Find these things in the picture:
  a computer
  a guitar
  a pan
  a spaceship
- Work with a friend. Imagine you are hiding in the town. Ask your friend to guess where you are hiding.
  e.g. *Are you in a building?*
- Translate the names of the buildings. Which words are the same in your language?

BUILDINGS

1 airport
2 bank
3 café
4 church
5 city hall
6 factory

7 gas station
8 hospital
9 hotel
10 market
11 movie theatre
12 museum

13 office building
14 parking garage
15 police station
16 post office
17 restaurant
18 store
19 supermarket/ grocery store
20 theatre
21 train station

- bus stop
- crosswalk
- lamppost
- mailbox
- road
- road sign
- sidewalk
- telephone booth
- traffic lights

The Country

1	bridge	7	grass	13	river
2	canal	8	highway	14	stream
3	cave	9	hill	15	tunnel
4	field	10	lake	16	valley
5	forest	11	mountain	17	waterf
6	garbage dump	12	reservoir		

- How many different animals are there in the picture?
- Find 8 things beginning with the letter **s**.
- Find these things in the picture:
  - **a fire**
  - **a hammock**
  - **a nest**
  - **a scarecrow**
  - **a rock**
- What is the difference between a mountain and a hill?

 backpack

 barn

 bush

 farmhouse

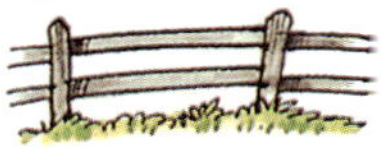 fence

 fire

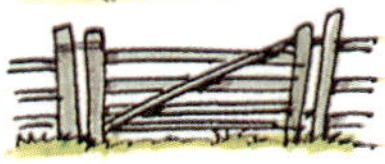 gate

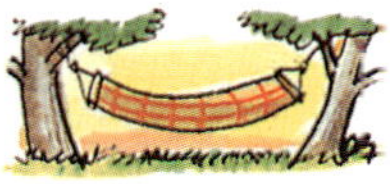 hammock

 haystack

 leaves

 litter/garbage

 nest

 picnic

 pylon

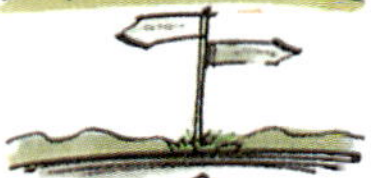 road sign

 rock

 scarecrow

 smoke

 stick

 tent

 tractor

 tree

The Beach

 bucket

 crab

 deckchair

 feather

 island

 lighthouse

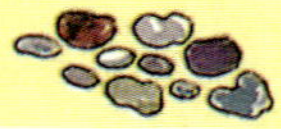 pebbles

 rocks

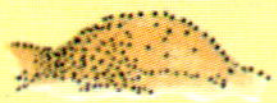 sand

 sand castle

 seaweed

 shells

 spade

 starfish

 sunglasses

 sunscreen

 surfboard

 waves

- Find these things in the pictures:

  flowers **a slide**
  goggles **a swing**

- Find 2 things that are in all 3 pictures.
- Find a picture of the seaside or a swimming pool in a magazine. Stick the picture on a sheet of paper. Label the picture.

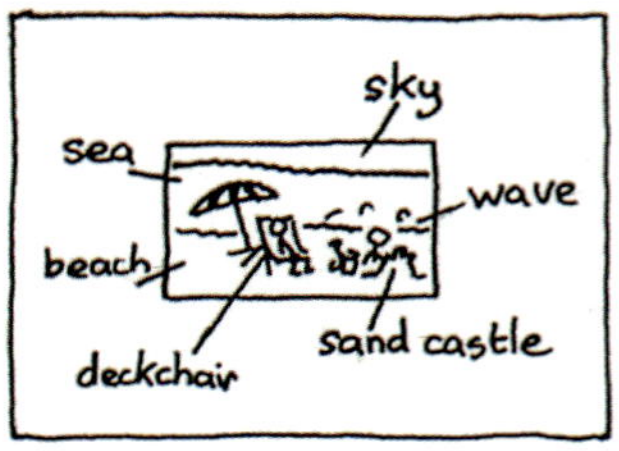

The Park

The Swimming Pool

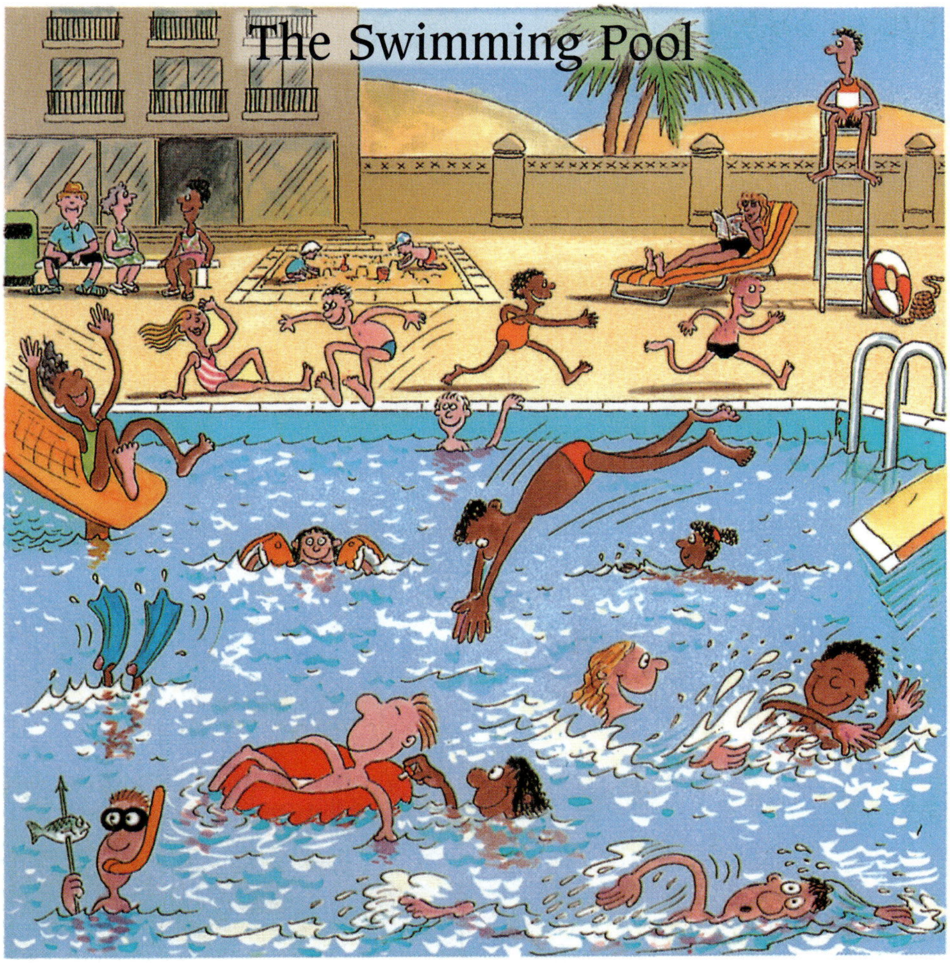

 bench

 diving board

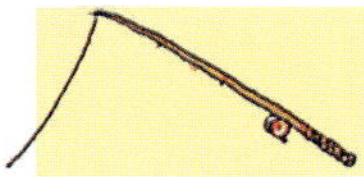 fishing rod

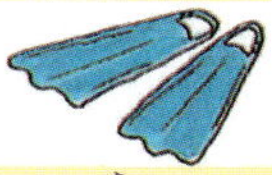 flippers

 flower

 fountain

 garbage can

 goggles

 lifeguard

 lifesaver

 merry-go-round

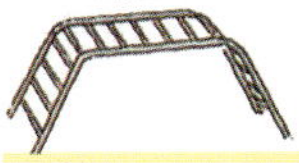 monkey bars

 pond

 rope

 sandbox

 seesaw

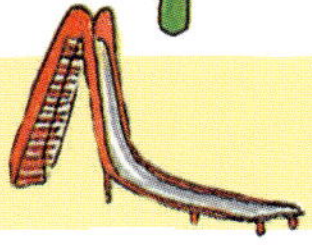 slide

 snorkel

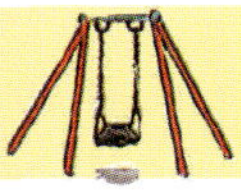 swing

 water

 water wings

 wheelbarrow

When I grow up . . .

1 actor 2 actress

actor

3 artist

4 bank clerk

10 doctor

11 electrician

12 firefighter

16 nurse

17 pilot

18 plumber

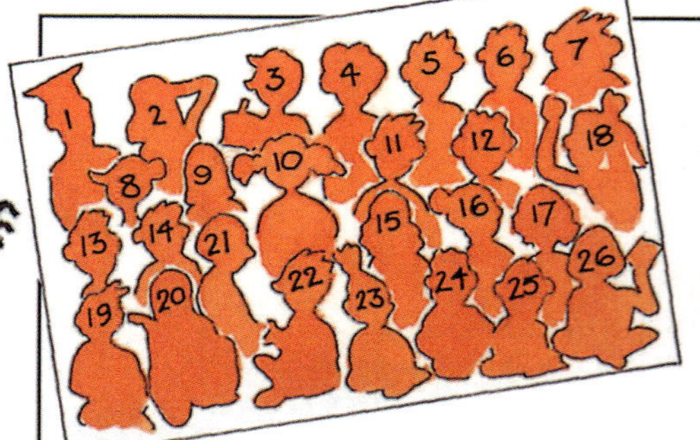

21 scientist

22 secretary

23 singer

■ What are these things called in English? Who uses them?

bus driver

6 chef

7 construction worker

8 dancer

9 dentist

13 hairdresser

14 letter carrier

15 mechanic

19 police officer

20 sales clerk

- Rearrange the letters to make words.

  redcan **crsaeyetr**
  etv **mlbrpue**

- Work with a friend. Point to a boy or a girl in the picture. Ask your friend:
  What does he want to be?
  What does she want to be?
- What do you want to be? Ask your friends.

24 vet

25 waiter

26 waitress

waiter

Once upon a time . . .

- Find 4 things beginning with the letter **c**.
- How many **crowns** are there in the picture?
- Are these sentences true or false?

The giant is holding an axe.
The skeleton is flying on the broomstick.
The dragon is red.
The pirate is wearing a crown.

STORYBOOK CHARACTERS

1 alien
2 dragon
3 fairy
4 genie
5 ghost
6 giant
7 king
8 mermaid
9 monster
10 pirate
11 prince
12 princess
13 queen
14 skeleton
15 vampire
16 witch
17 wizard

axe
broomstick
castle
cottage
crown
moon
palace
sword
treasure
wand

The Calendar

December

Sunday	1 first	8 eighth	15 fifteenth	22 twenty-second	29 twenty-ninth
Monday	2 second	9 ninth	16 sixteenth	23 twenty-third	30 thirtieth
Tuesday	3 third	10 tenth	17 seventeenth	24 twenty-fourth	31 thirty-first
Wednesday	4 fourth	11 eleventh	18 eighteenth	25 twenty-fifth	
Thursday	5 fifth	12 twelfth	19 nineteenth	26 twenty-sixth	
Friday	6 sixth	13 thirteenth	20 twentieth	27 twenty-seventh	
Saturday	7 seventh	14 fourteenth	21 twenty-first	28 twenty-eighth	

1st first — 2nd second — 3rd third — 4th fourth

MONTHS

- January
- February
- March
- April
- May
- June
- July
- August
- September
- October
- November
- December

Mon	1	8	15	22	29
Tue	2	9	16	23	30
Wed	3	10	17	24	31
Thur	4	11	18	25	
Fri	5	12	19	26	
Sat	6	13	20	27	
Sun	7	14	21	28	

WHAT TIME IS IT?

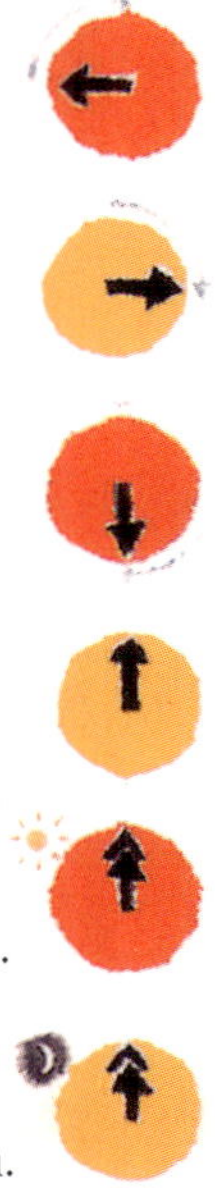

quarter to...

quarter past...

...thirty/
half past

...o'clock

p.m. noon

a.m. midnight

60 seconds	=	1 minute
60 minutes	=	1 hour
24 hours	=	1 day
7 days	=	1 week
52 weeks	=	1 year

morning

06:00–12:00

afternoon

12:00–18:00

evening

18:00–24:00

night

24:00–06:00

- What time is it?

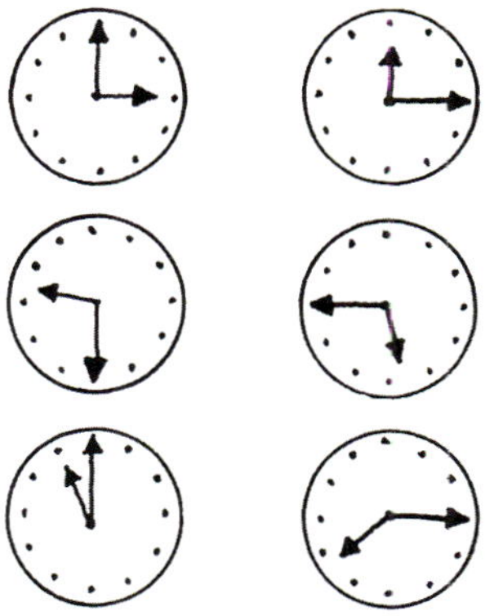

- Write the days of the week in alphabetical order.
- Say the months in English backwards.
- What is the date today?
- What was the date yesterday?
- When is your birthday? Draw a graph with your friends' birthdays.

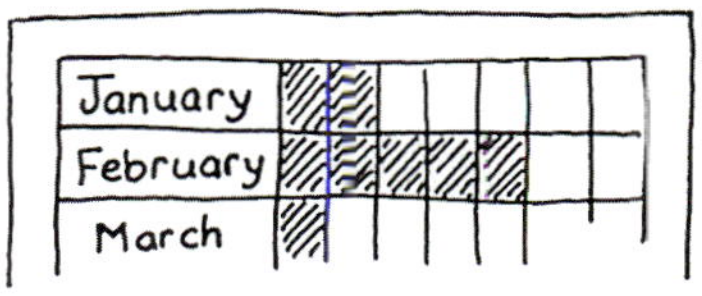

Beautiful or Ugly?

- Find 4 words beginning with the letter **c**.
- Say a word. Ask your friend to say the opposite.
- Which words mean the same?

closed	**big**
difficult	**hard**
large	**little**
loud	**noisy**
small	**shut**

- Which words describe each picture?

cold **long**
fat **sharp**
light

blunt
sharp
cheap
$1
$100000
expensive
clean
5
5
dirty
dark
light
easy
1+1 =
194·206
÷ 37·451
difficult/hard
empty
full
fast
slow
fat
thin
healthy
ill
heavy
light
here
there
high
low
noisy/loud
ROAR!
Eek!
quiet
old
young
open
closed
rich
poor
strong
weak
thick
thin
top
bottom
wet
dry

Where is it?

above

The rat is **above** the hat.

The birds are **above** the words.

behind

The fox is **behind** the rocks.

The frog is sitting **behind** the dog.

between

The fox is **between** the rocks.

down

The bears are walking **down** the stairs.

in

There is a mouse **in** the house.

The fish is **in** the dish.

in front of

The fox is **in front of** the rocks.

The frog is sitting **in front of** the dog.

into

The slug is crawling **into** the jug.

near

The cat is **near** the rat.

Where are the frogs?

next to/by

The rat is **next to** the hat.

on

The cat is **on** the mat.

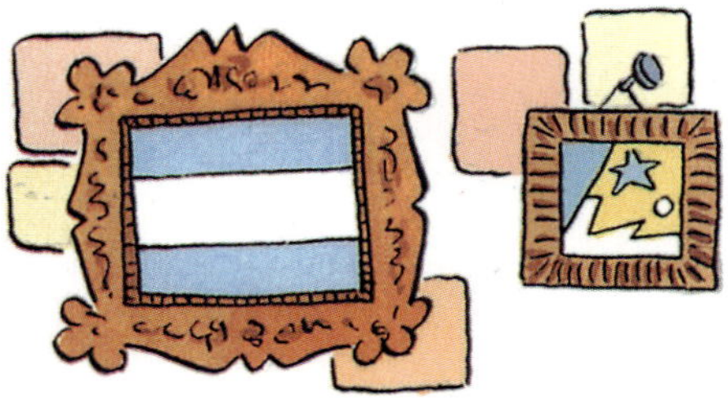

There are two pictures **on** the wall, one is big and one is small.

out of

There's a witch on a broom flying **out of** the room.

over

There's a snake crawling **over** the cake.

under

There is a hare **under** the chair.

The words are **under** the birds.

up

The bears are walking **up** the stairs.

- Find 3 things beginning with the letter **f**.
- What are these?

c _ _

c _ _ _ _

c _ _ _ _

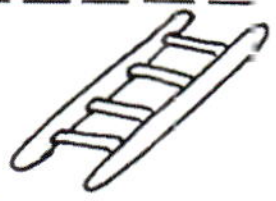

l _ _ _ _ _

c _ _ _

b _ _ _ _ _

- Work with a friend. Ask some questions about the frogs.
  e.g. *Where's the green frog?*
  Where's the blue frog?
  Is the red frog under the chair?
- **Fish** rhymes with **dish**
  Connect the words that rhyme.

birds	hair
chair	box
frog	words
rat	dog
rocks	hat

- Find 8 words in the puzzle.

downeinonunderbynerintoupnear

What's the weather like?

- Find these things in the pictures:

  a bucket
  a kite
  a glove
  sunglasses

- Copy the puzzle. Write the words.

Insects and Small Creatures

ant

bee

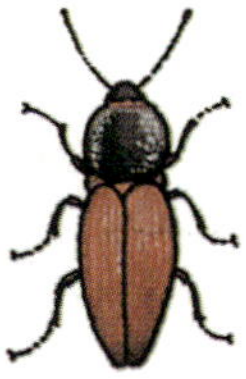
beetle

butterfly

caterpillar

centipede

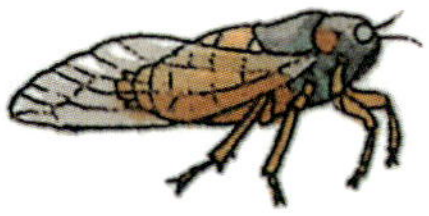
cicada

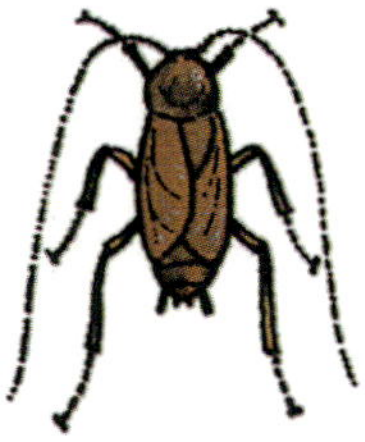
cockroach

cricket

dragonfly

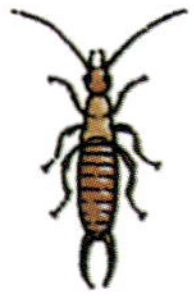
earwig

firefly

flea

fly

grasshopper

ladybug

locust

mantis

millipede

mosquito

moth

scorpion

slug

snail

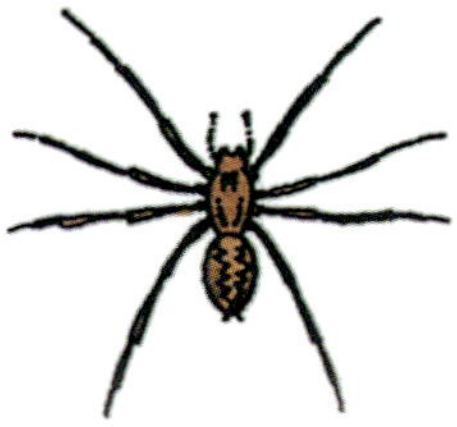
spider

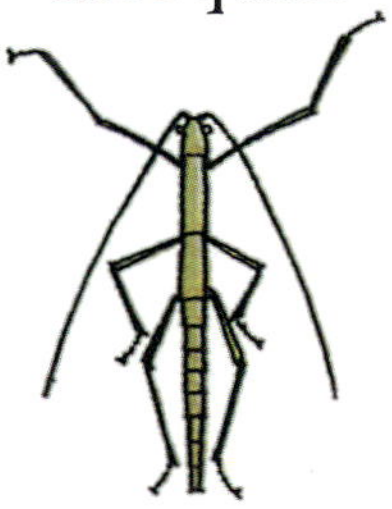
stick insect

wasp

woodlouse

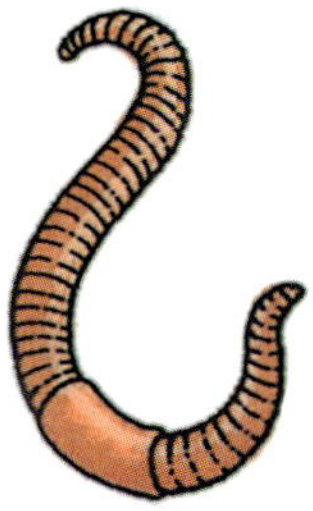
worm

- There is a small creature on every double page of this dictionary. Find the creatures. Which pages are they on?
- How many creatures on this page have wings?
- Rearrange the letters and make words.

  baglydu **lnsia**
  ugsl **aetclirplra**
  rcospoin **afle**
- Insects have 6 legs. Which of these creatures are not insects?

  ant **fly** **millipede** **snail**
  beetle **mantis** **slug** **spider**

Flags, Countries and Nationalities

Argentina
Argentinian

Australia
Australian

Austria
Austrian

Belgium
Belgian

Brazil
Brazilian

Canada
Canadian

Chile
Chilean

China
Chinese

Denmark
Danish

Finland
Finnish

France
French

Germany
German

Greece
Greek

India
Indian

Italy
Italian

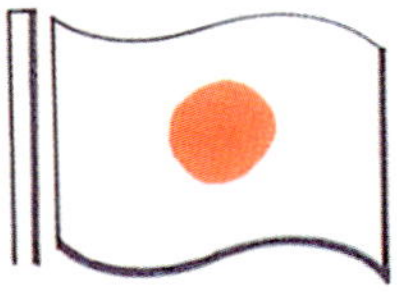

Japan
Japanese

Mexico
Mexican

New Zealand
New Zealand

Norway
Norwegian

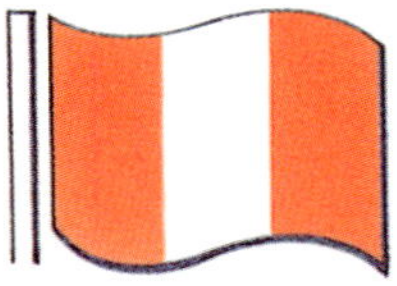

Peru
Peruvian

Russia
Russian

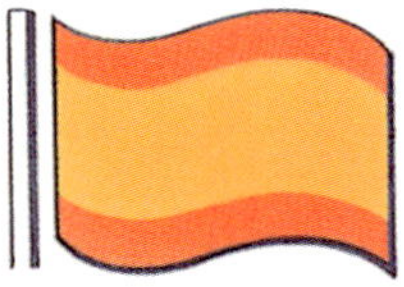

Spain
Spanish

Sweden
Swedish

Switzerland
Swiss

Thailand
Thai

Turkey
Turkish

The U.K.
British

The U.S.A.
American

Venezuela
Venezuelan

- There is a flag on every double page of this dictionary. Find the flags. Which pages are they on?
- How many flags are red, white and blue?
- Which flag is blue and yellow?
- How many stars are there on the Australian flag?
- Which flags are these?

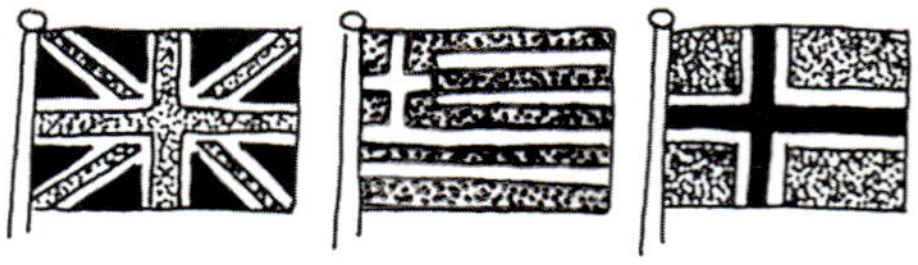

AaBbCcDdEeFfGgHhIiJjKkLlMm

Word List

The following pages contain an alphabetical list of all the words in the dictionary. Next to each word is the number of the page on which the word appears.

NnOoPpQqRrSsTtUuVvWwXxYyZz

a

b

C

d

e

f

g

h

i

j

k

l

m 

n 

o

p

q

r

s

AaBbCcDdEeFfGgHhIiJjKkLlMm

t

u

v

w

AaBbCcDdEeFfGgHhIiJjKkLlMm

NnOoPpQqRrSsTtUuVvWwXxYyZz